# CUT AND COLOR COOKIES

THEBLUEOFMYEYE
PUBLISHING

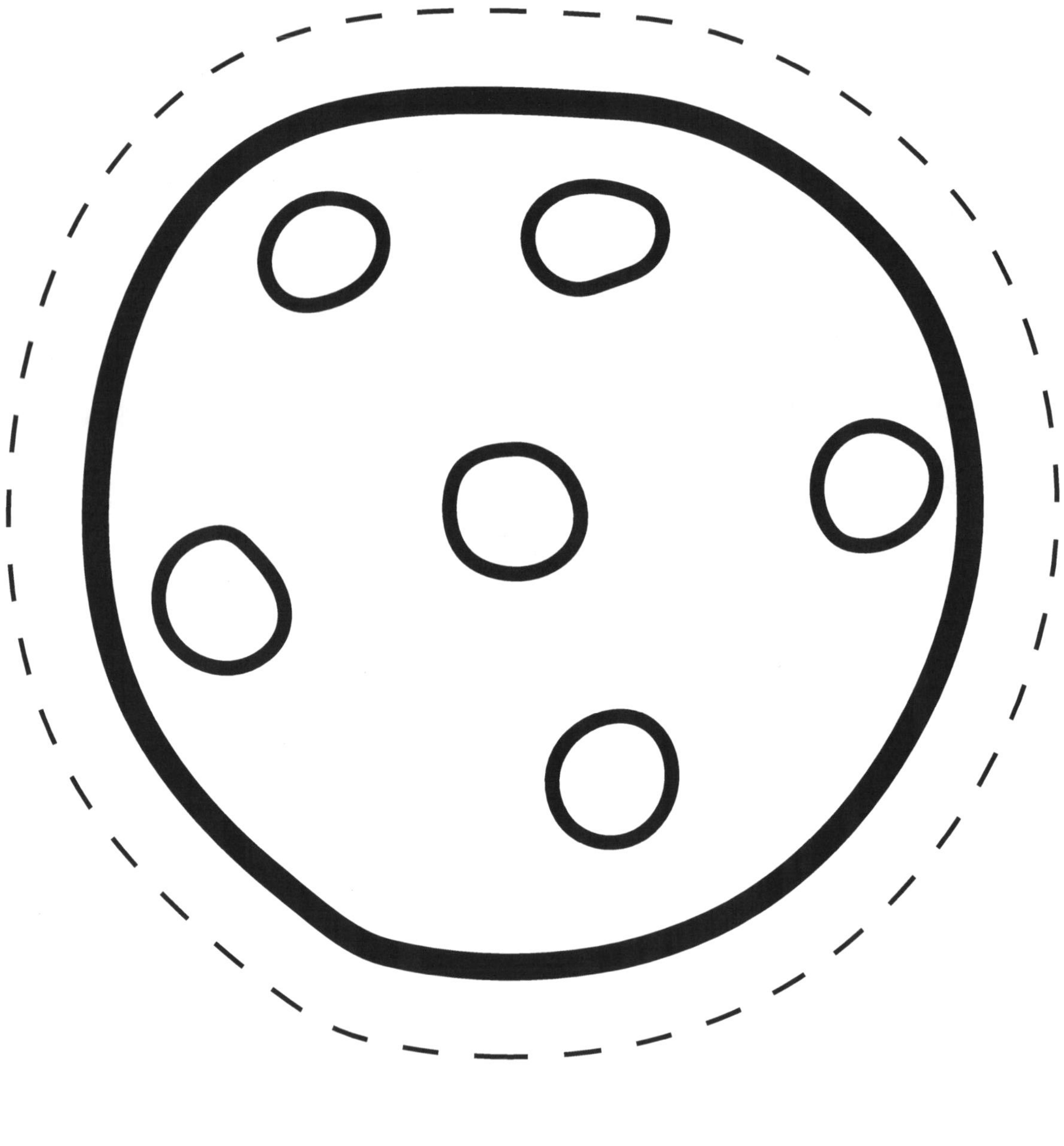

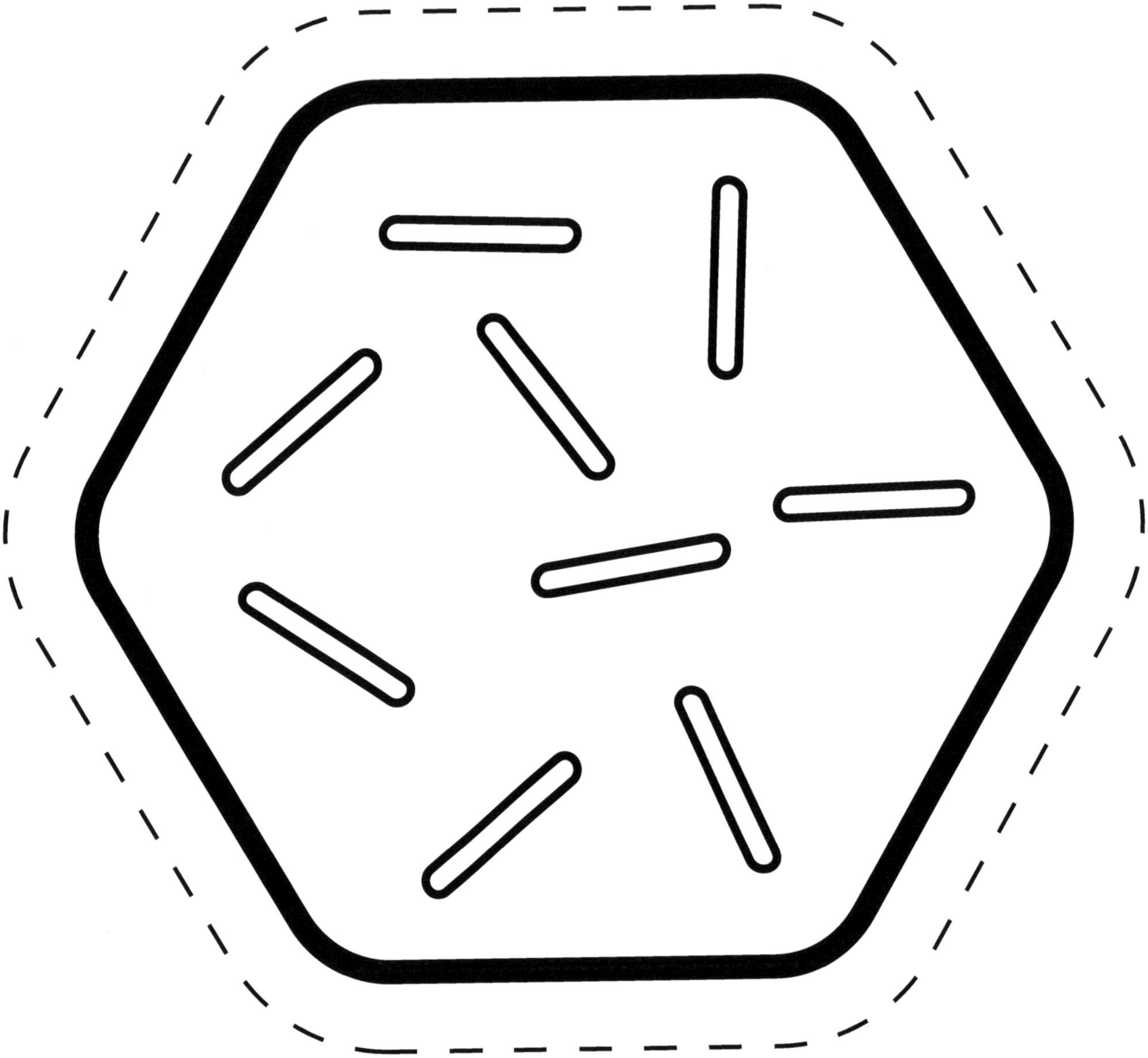

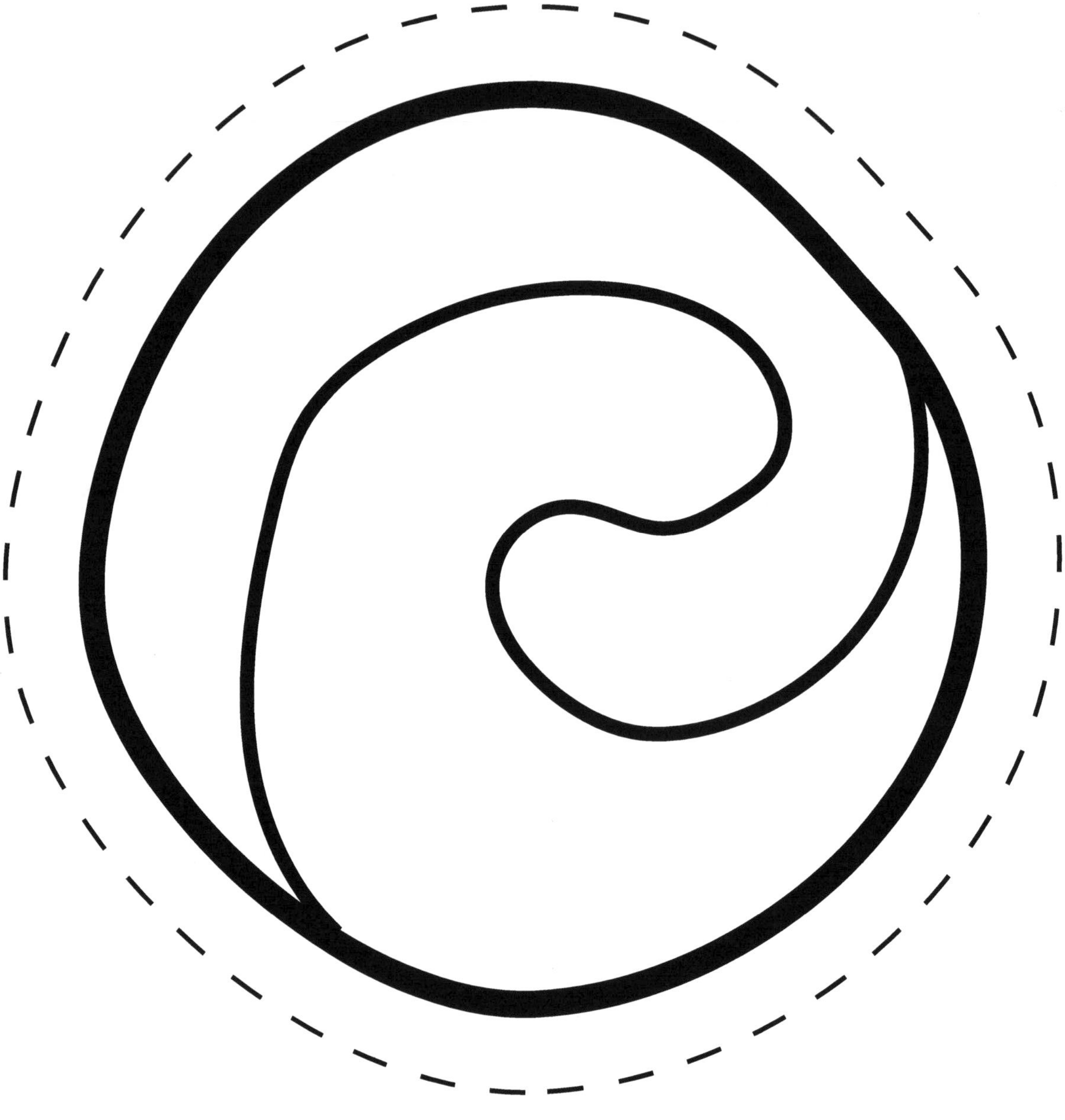

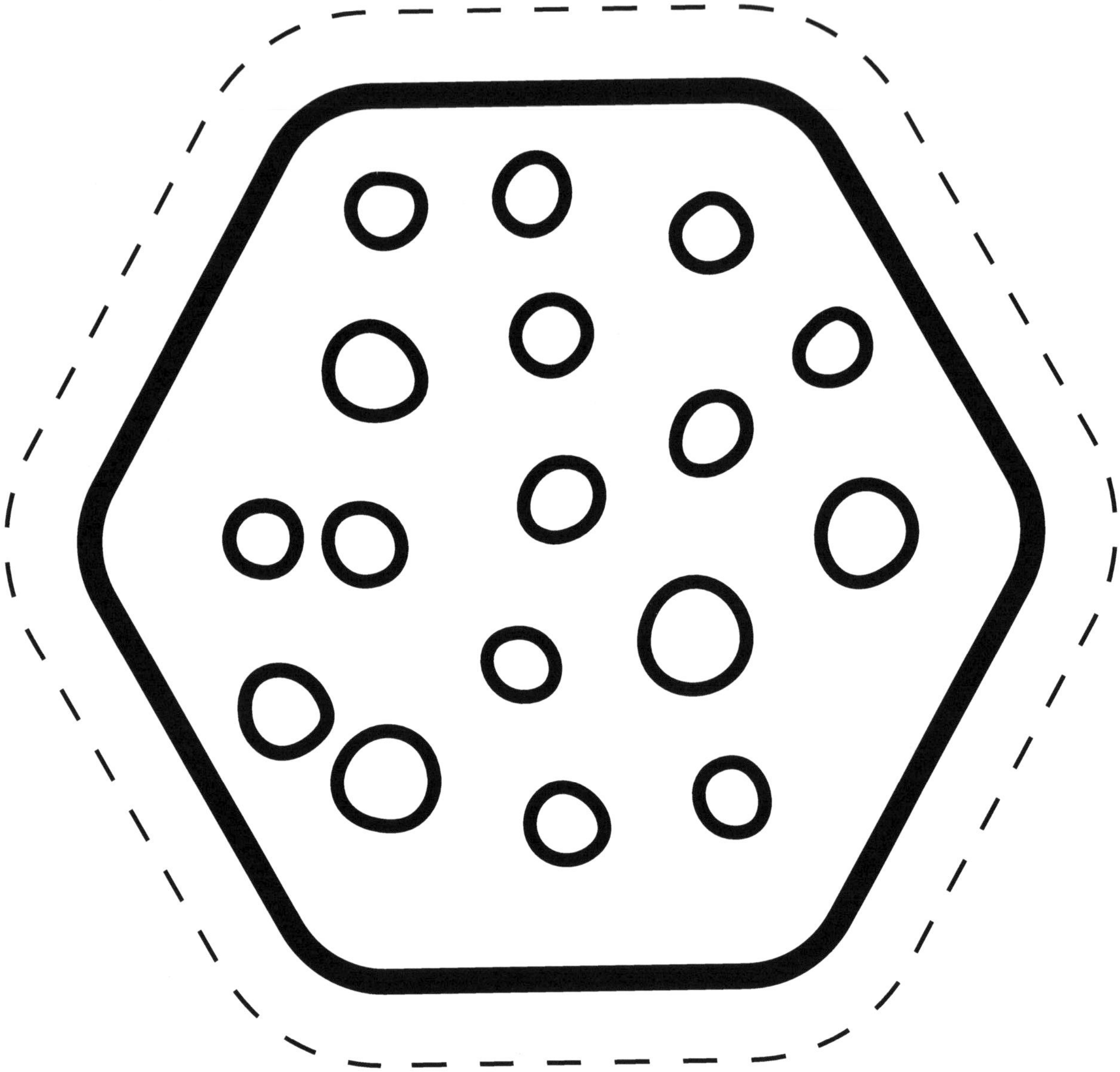

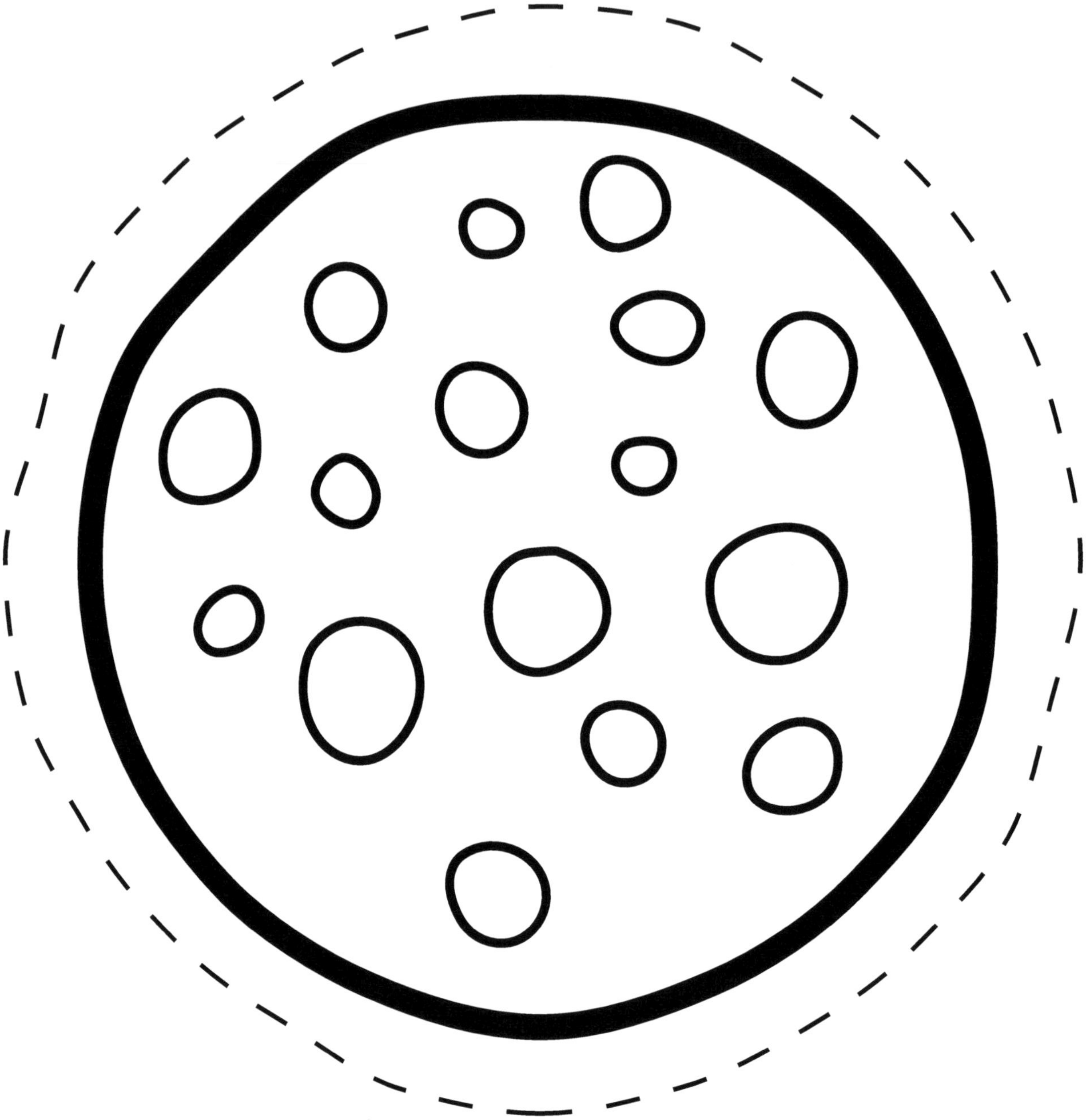

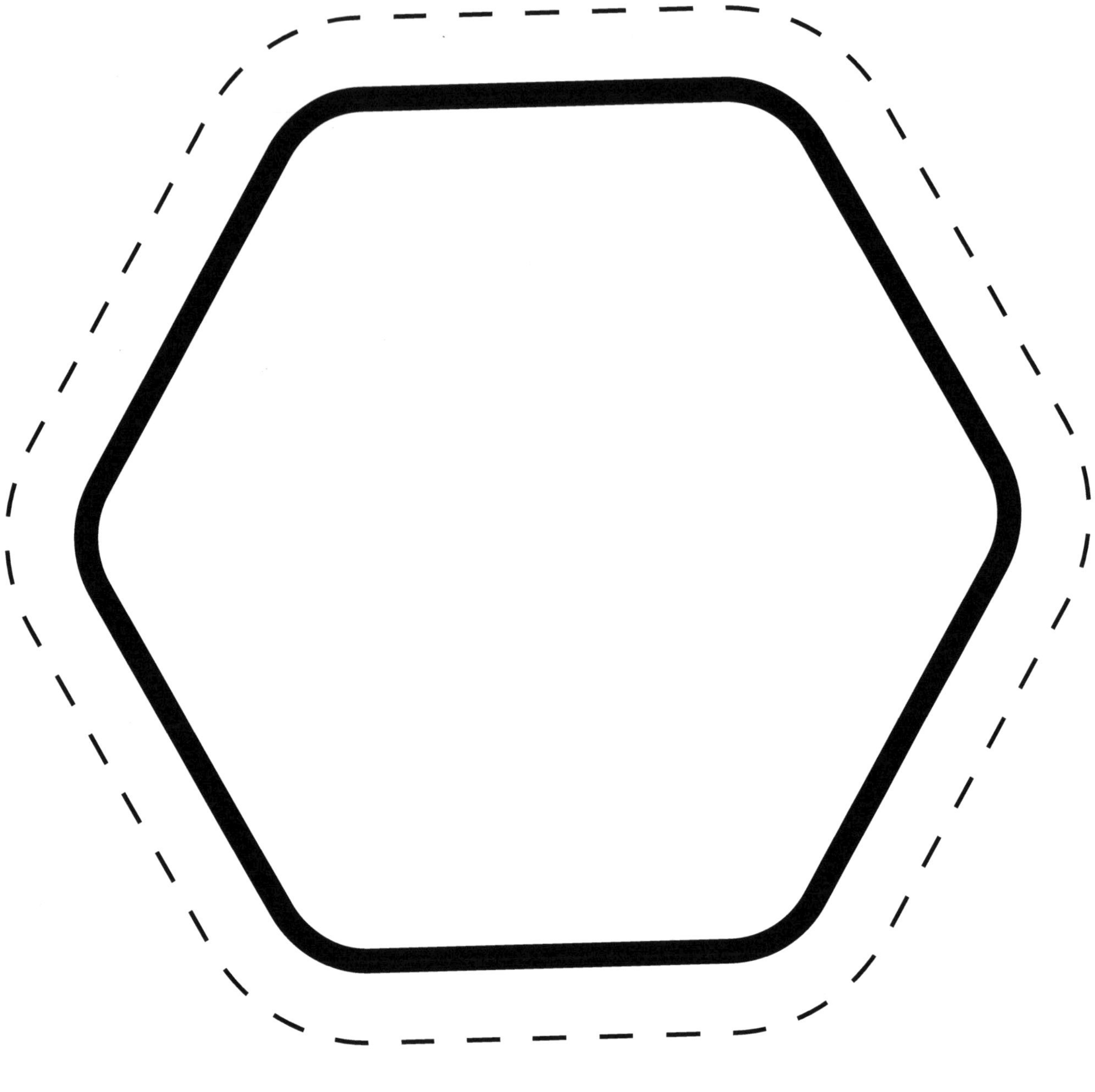

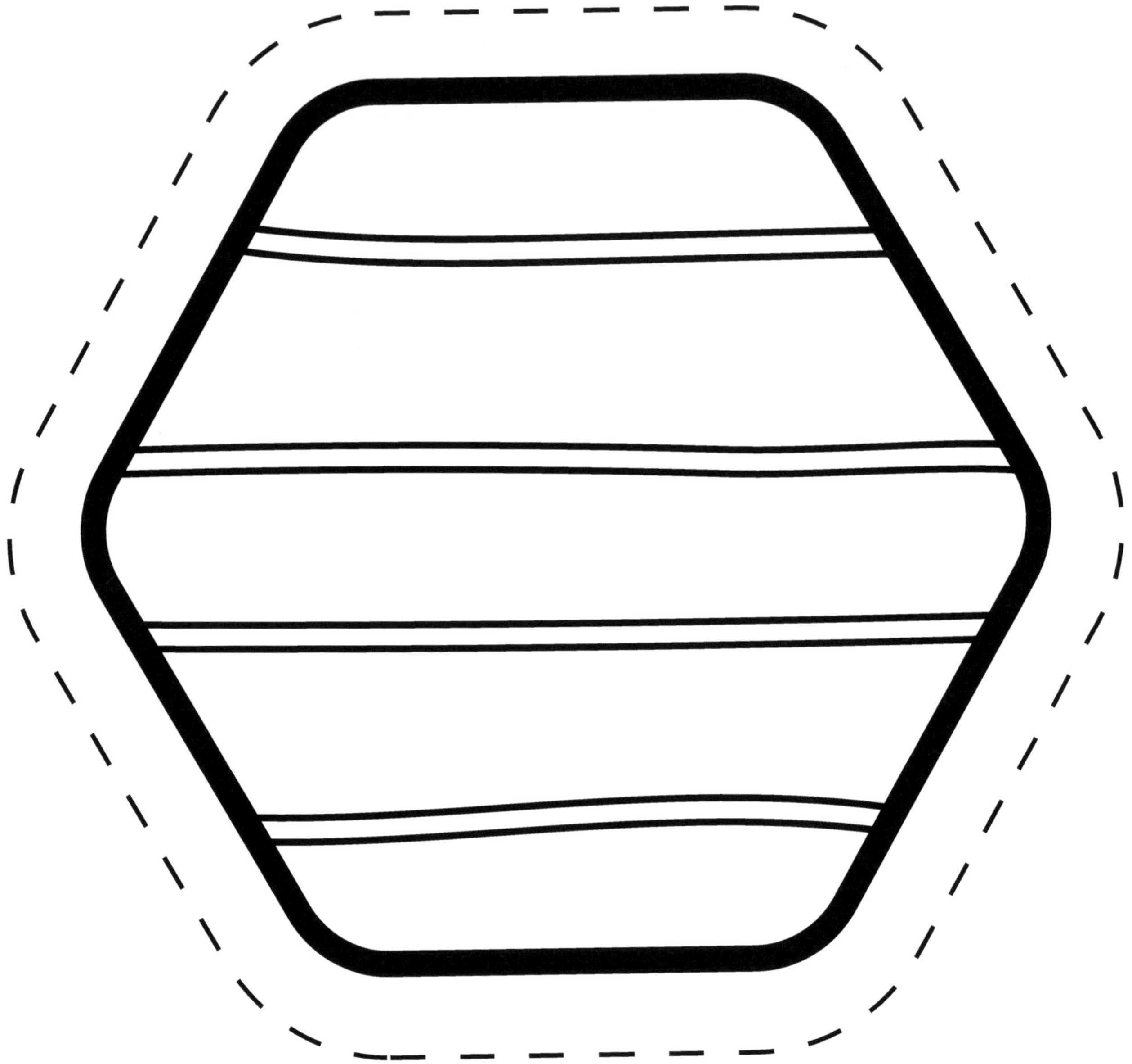

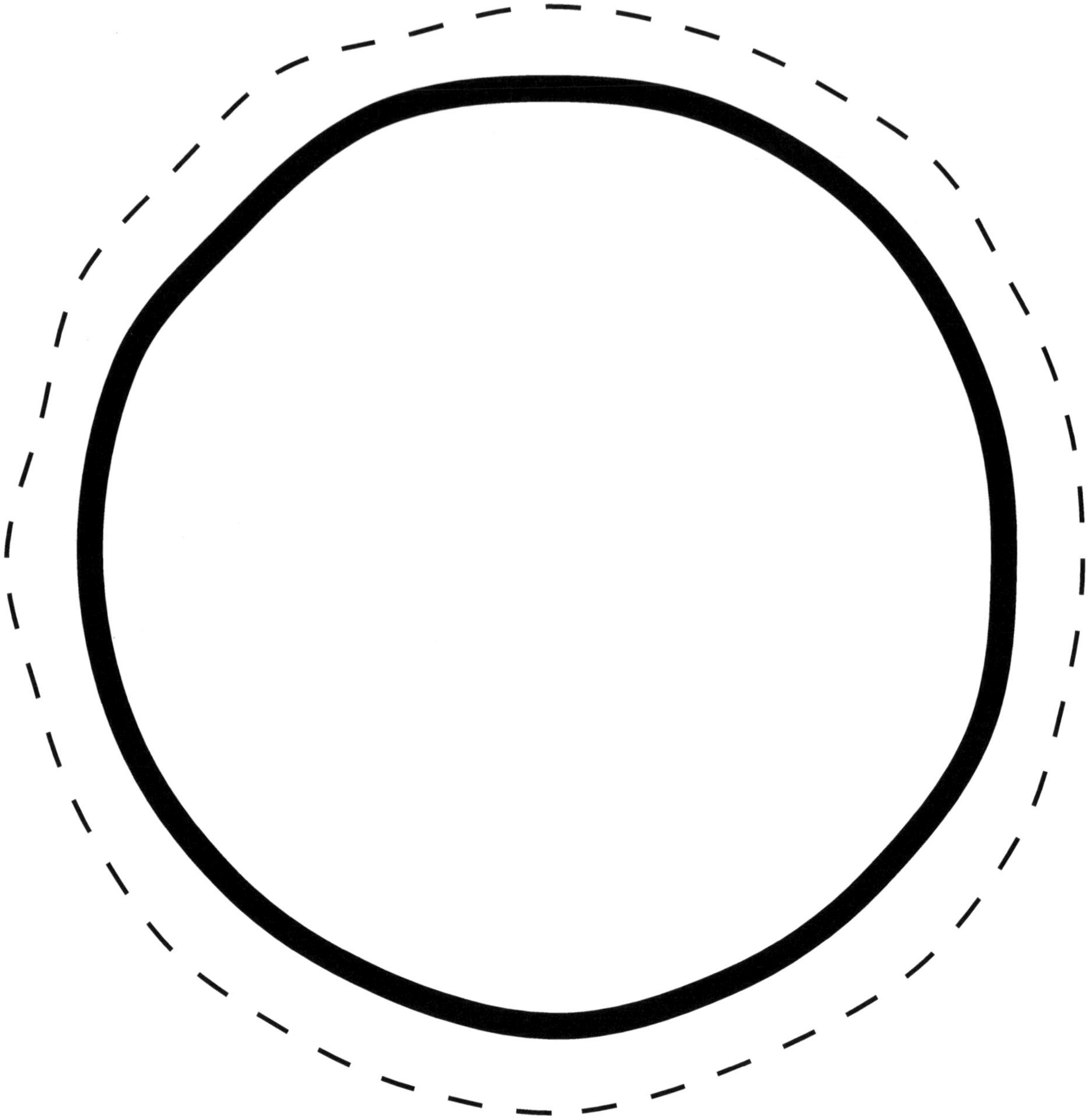

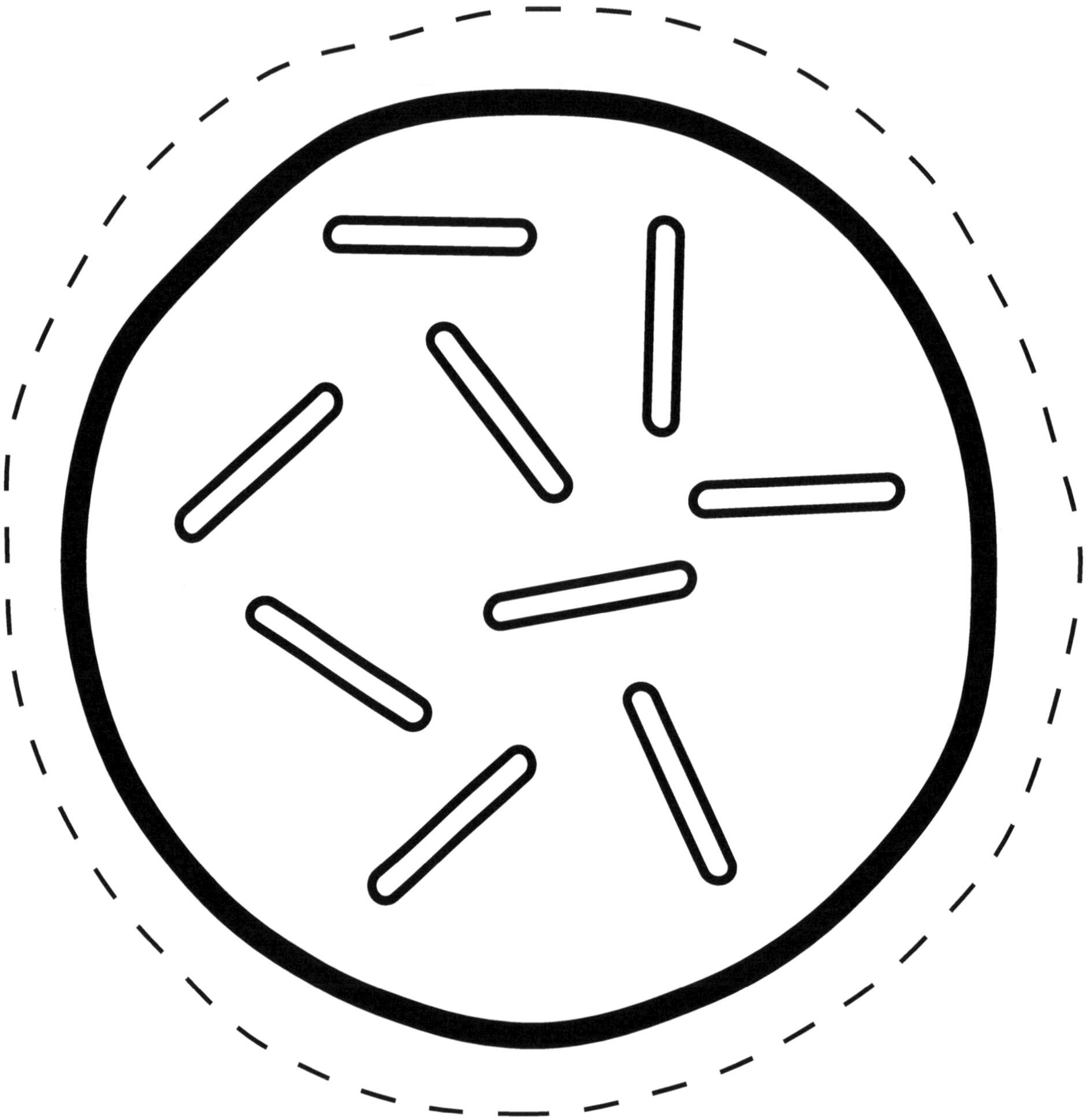

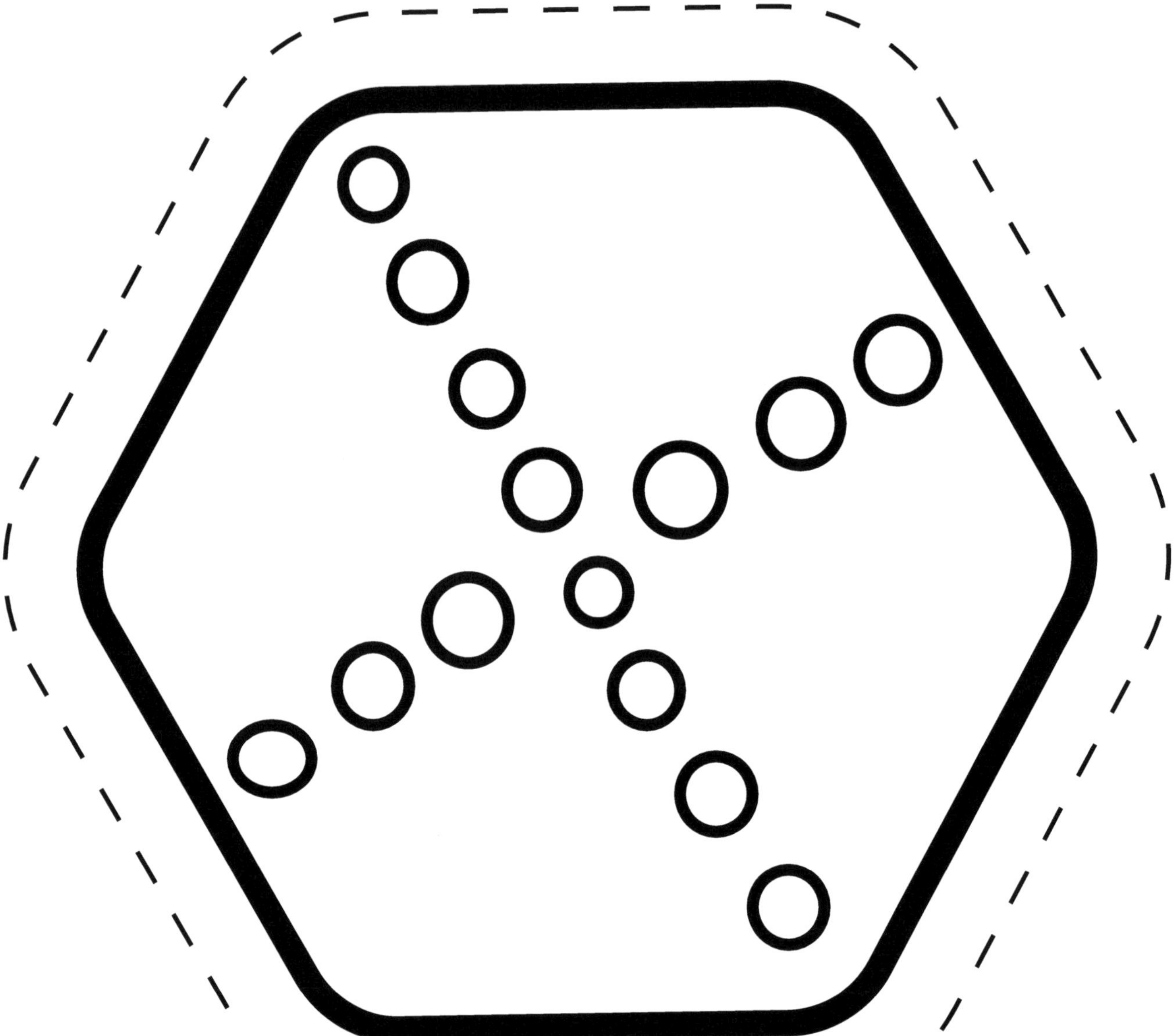

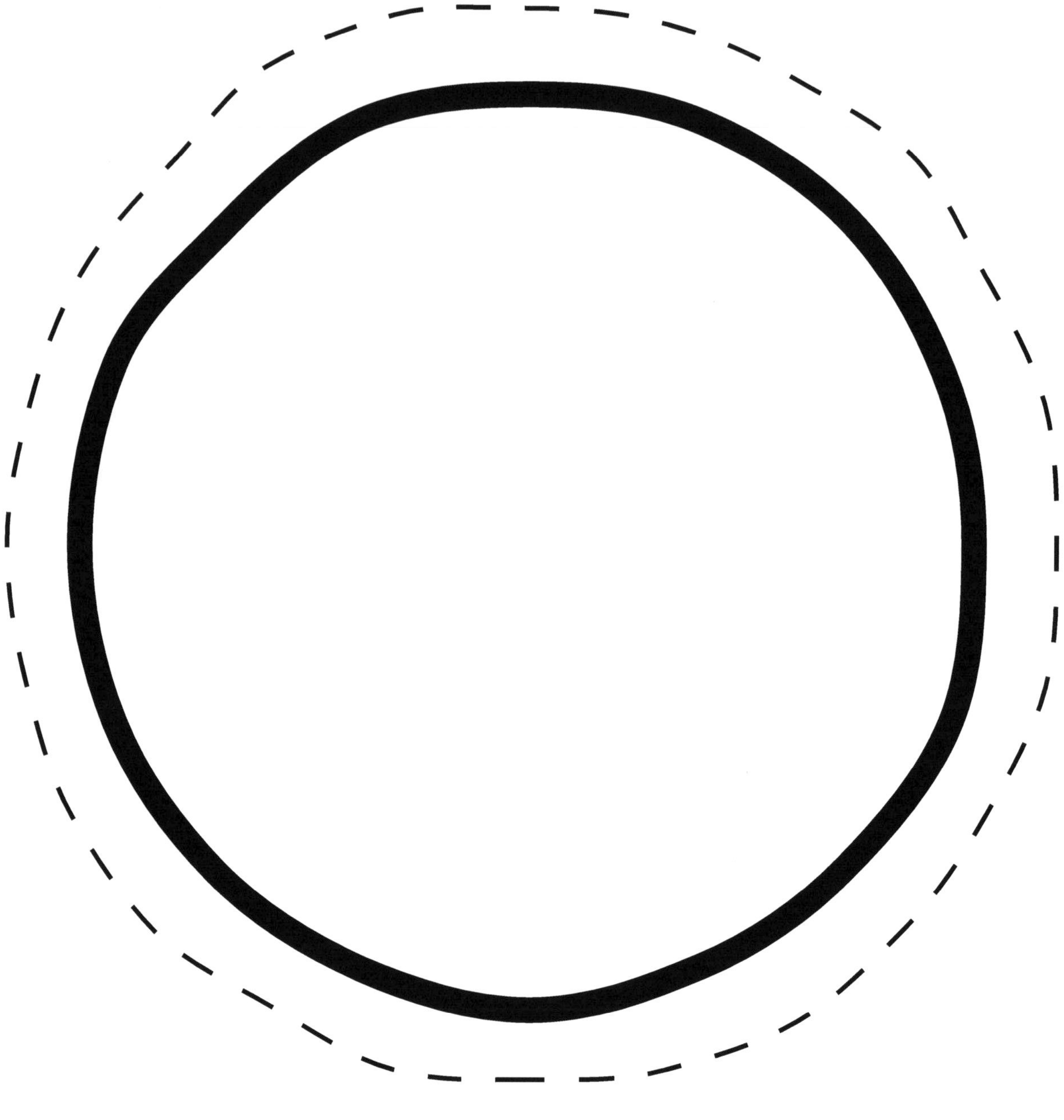

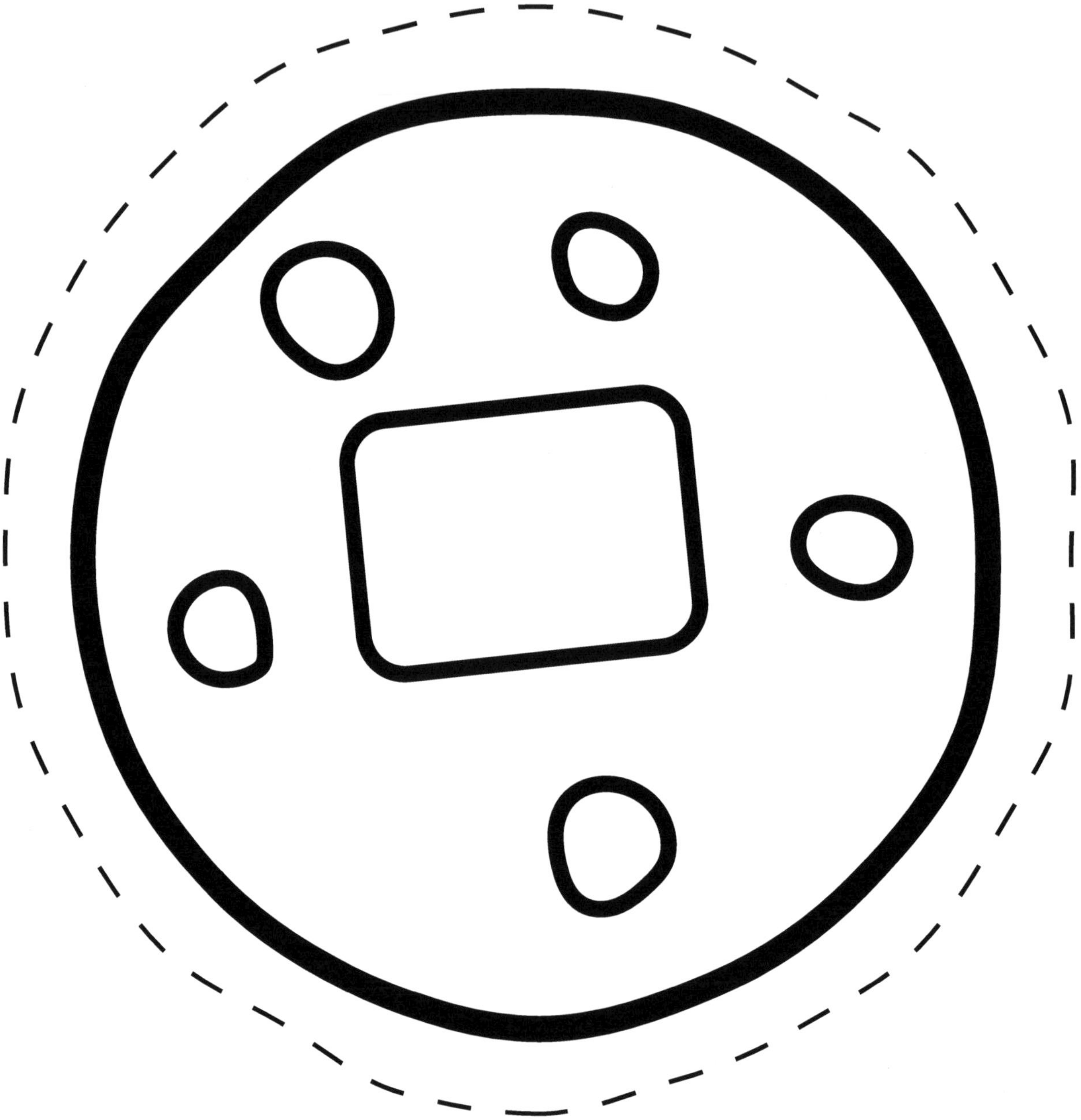

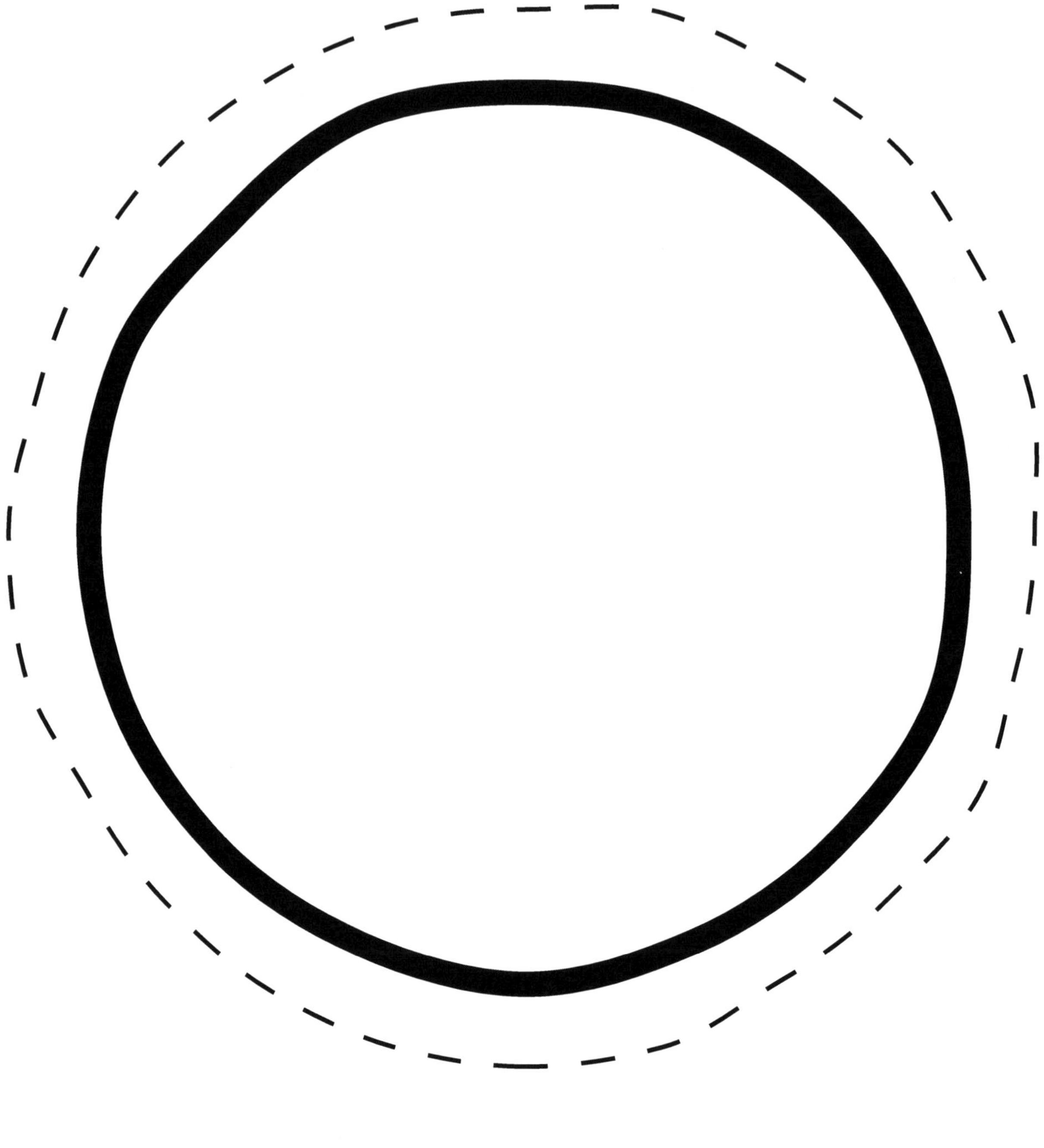

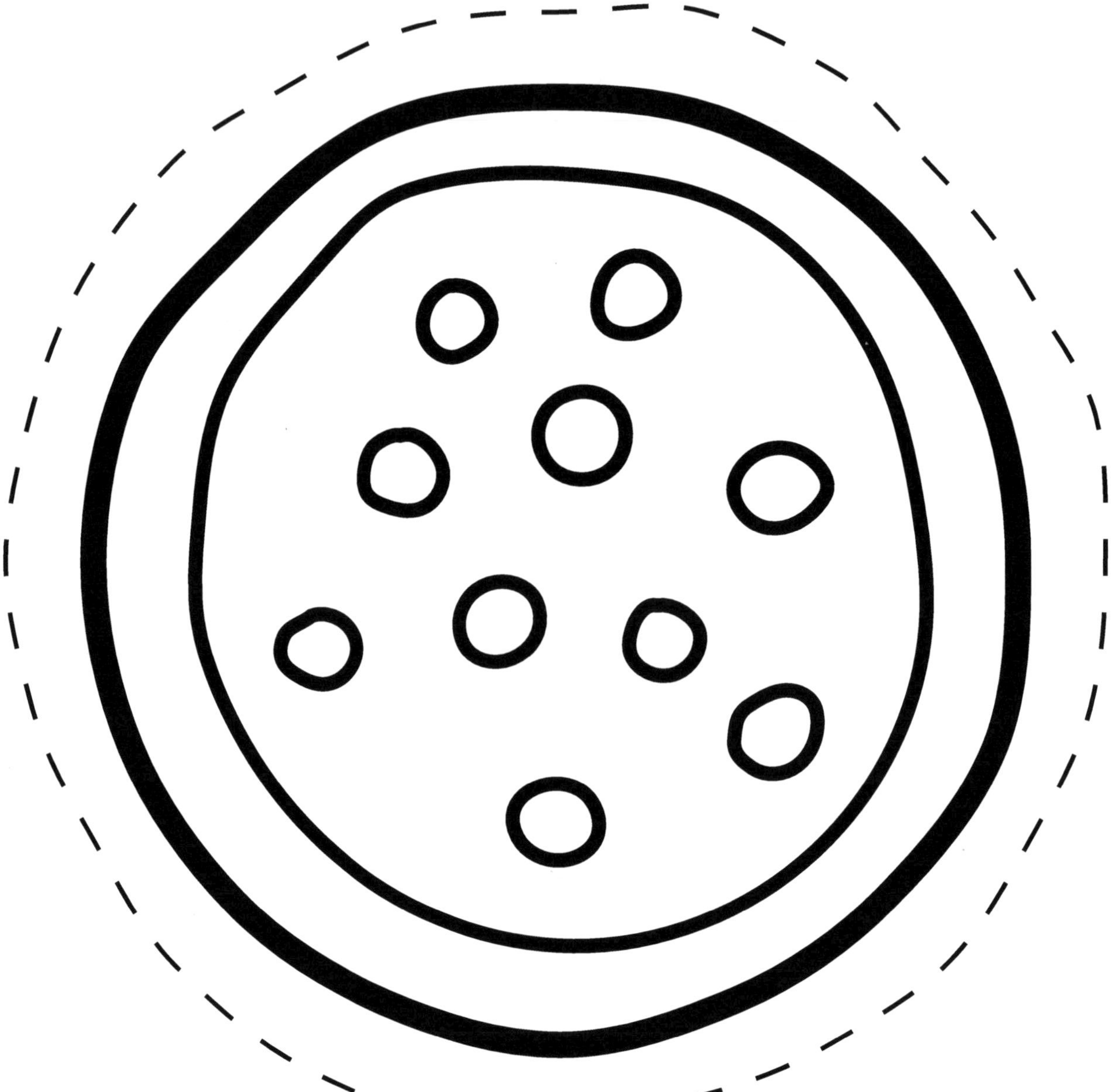

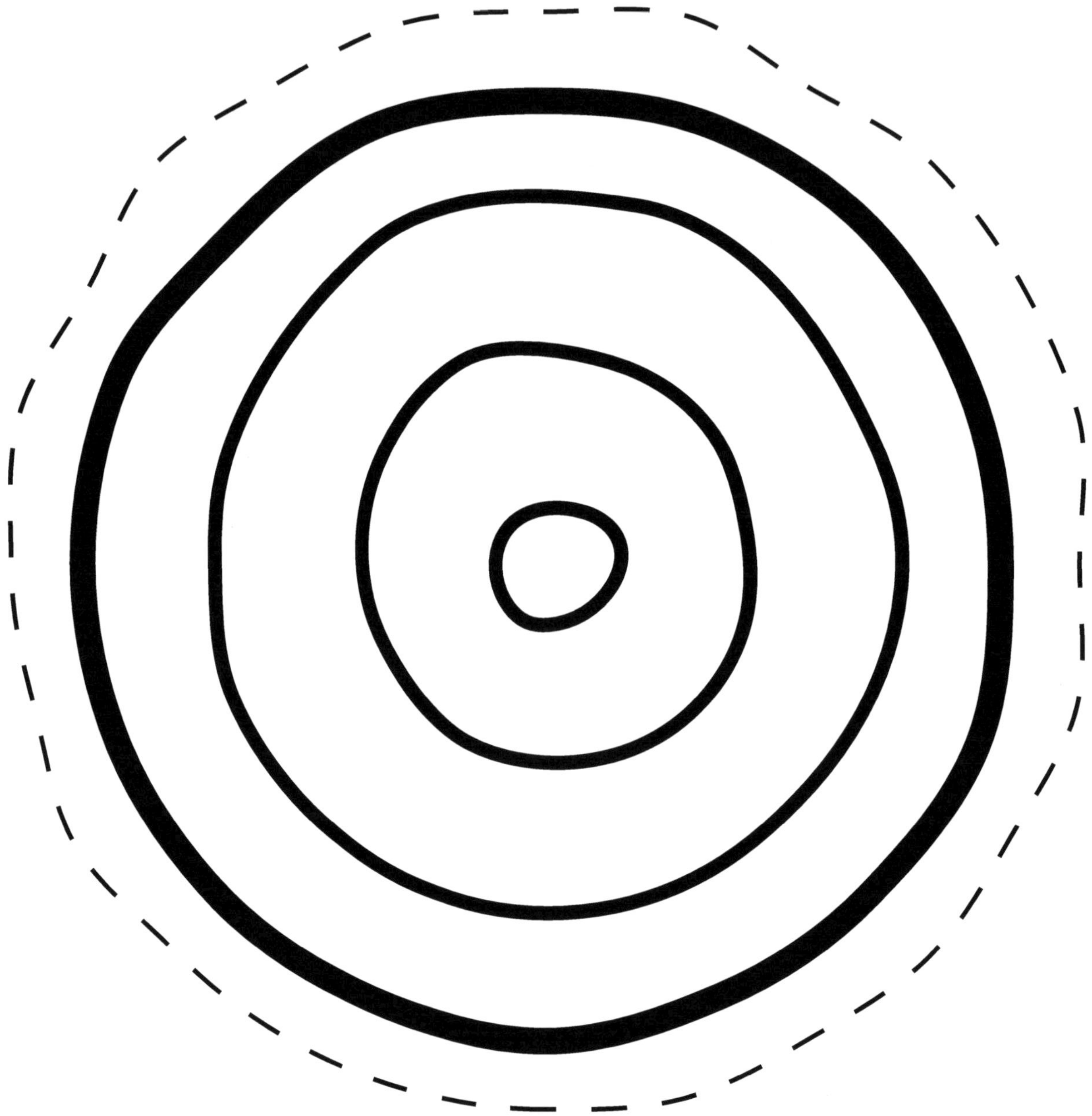

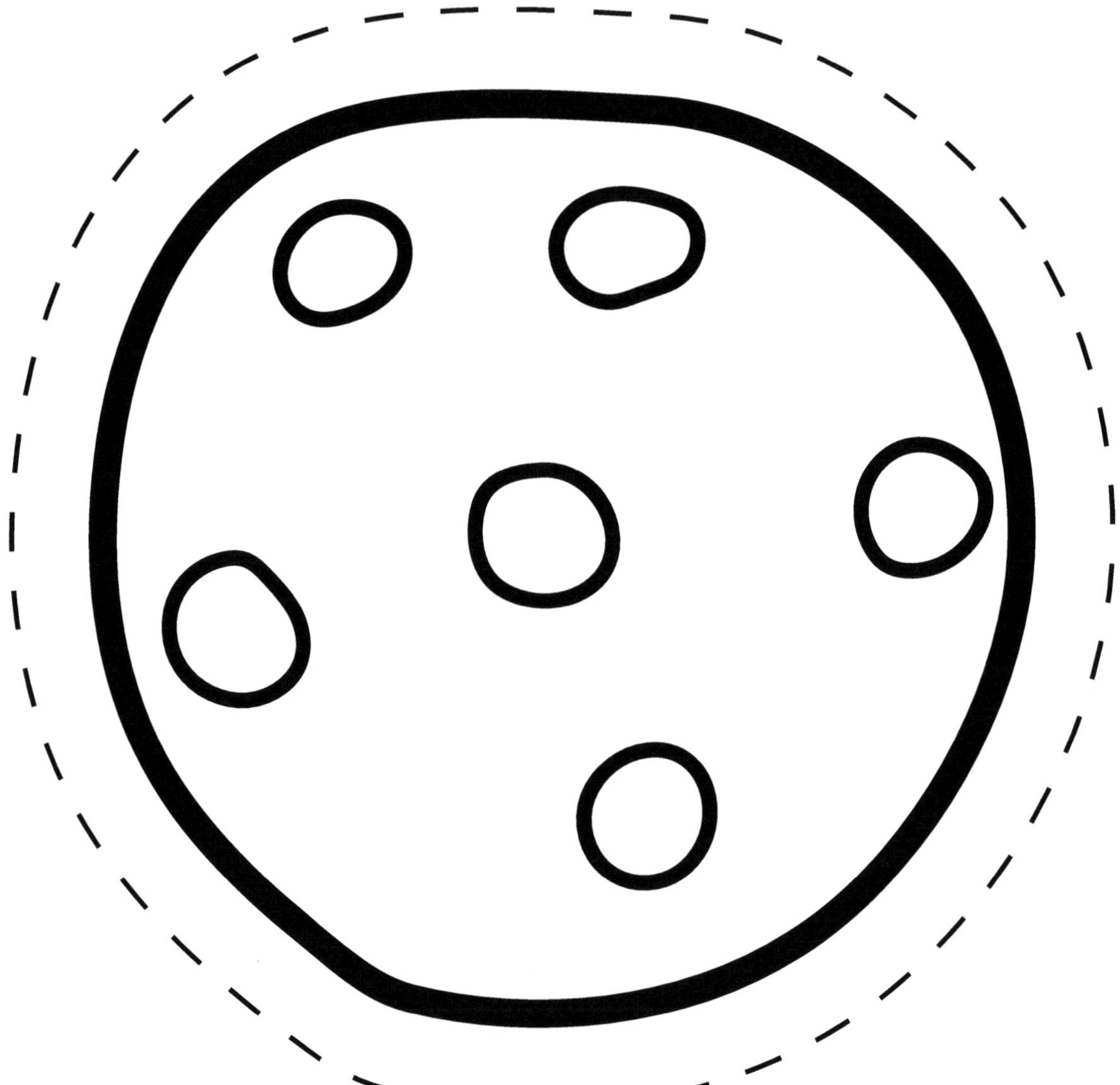

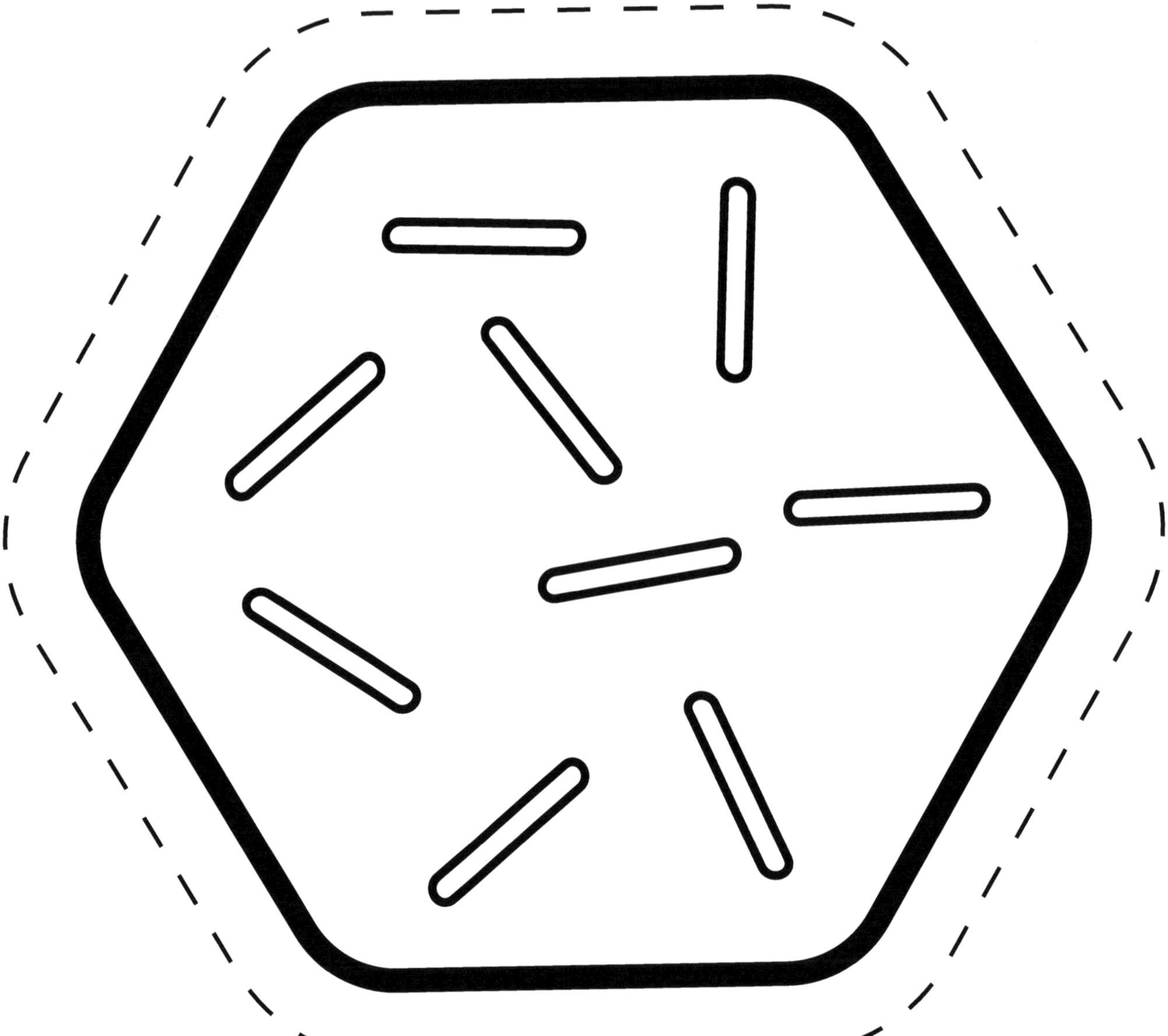

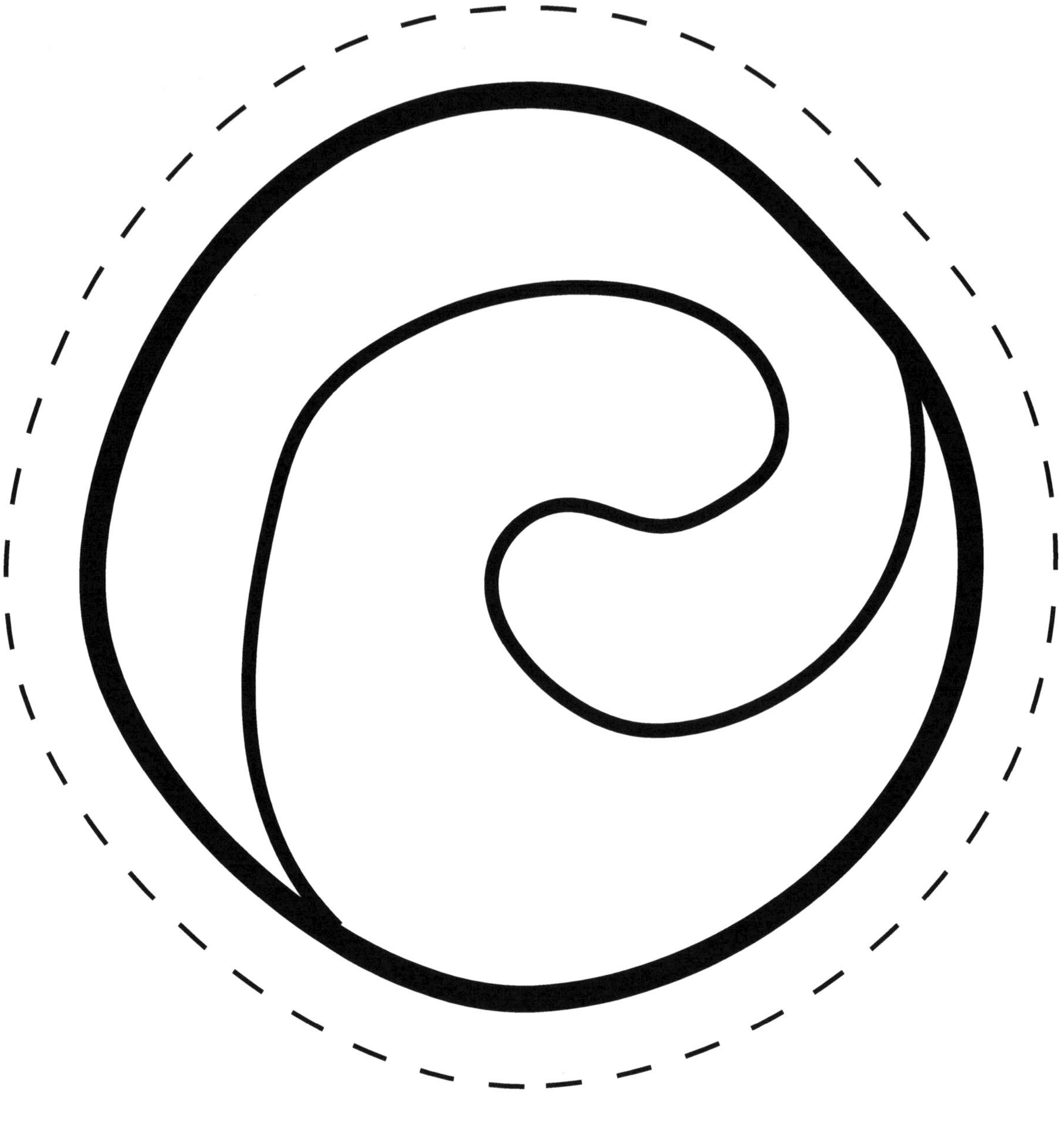

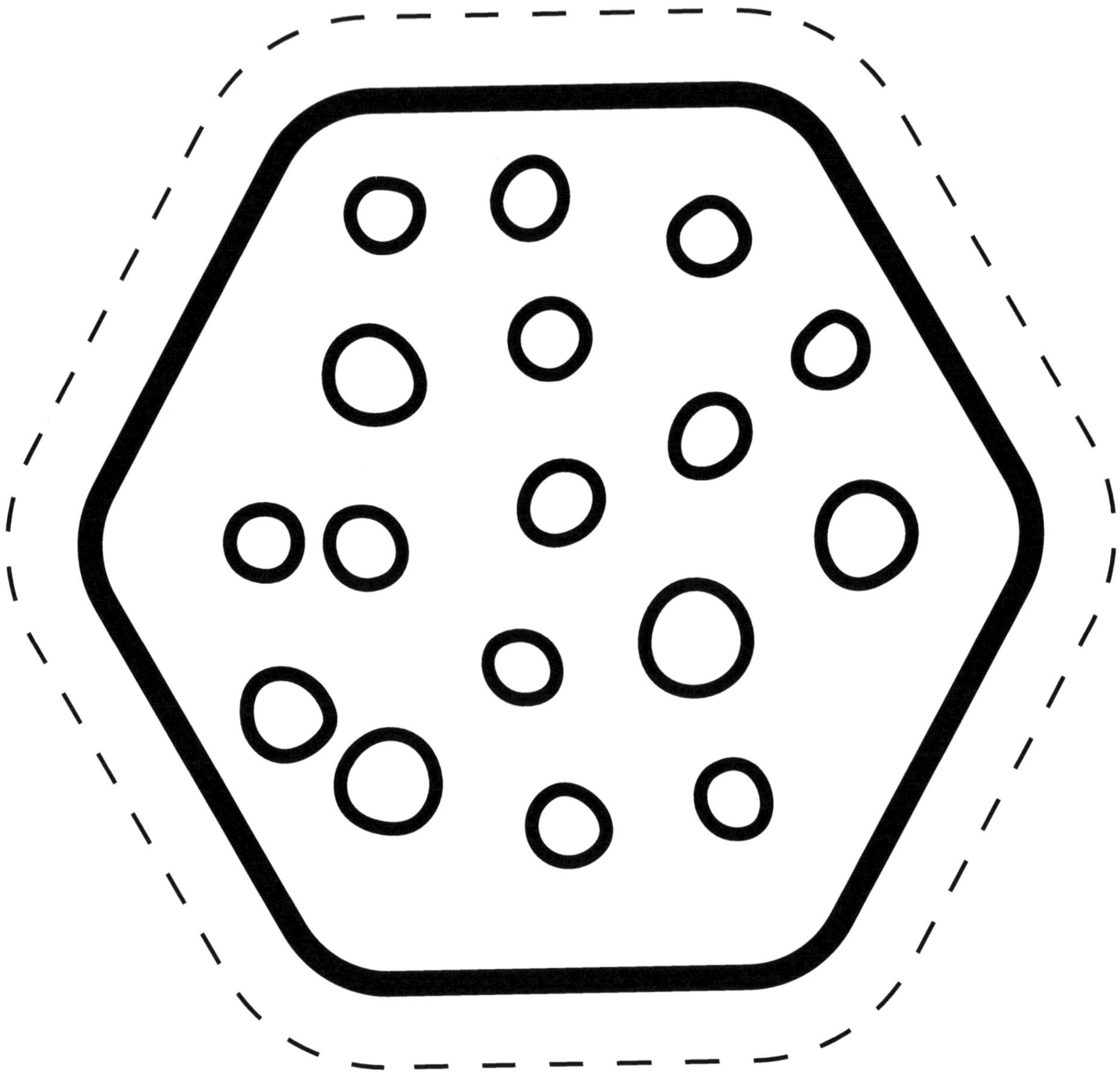

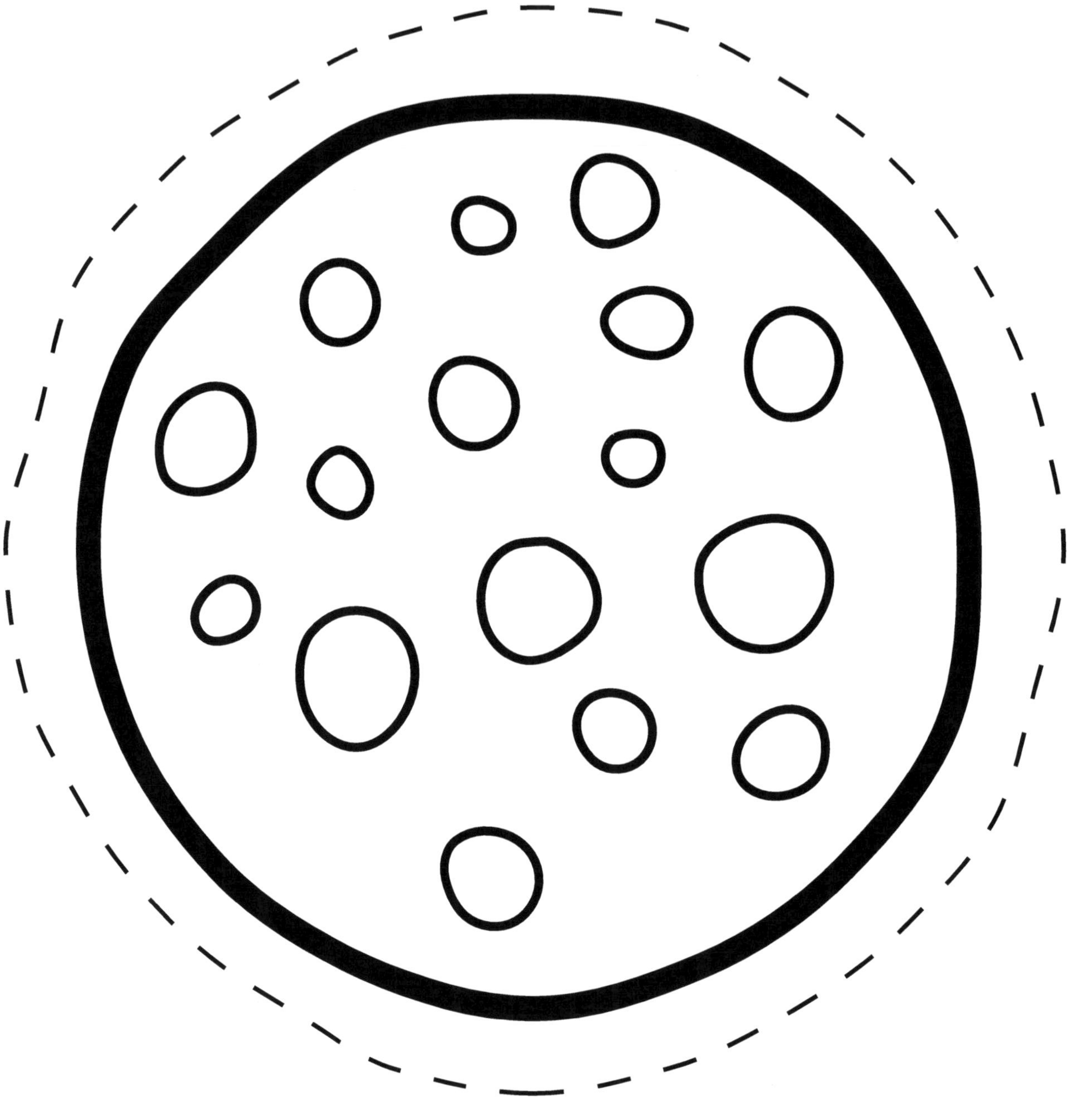

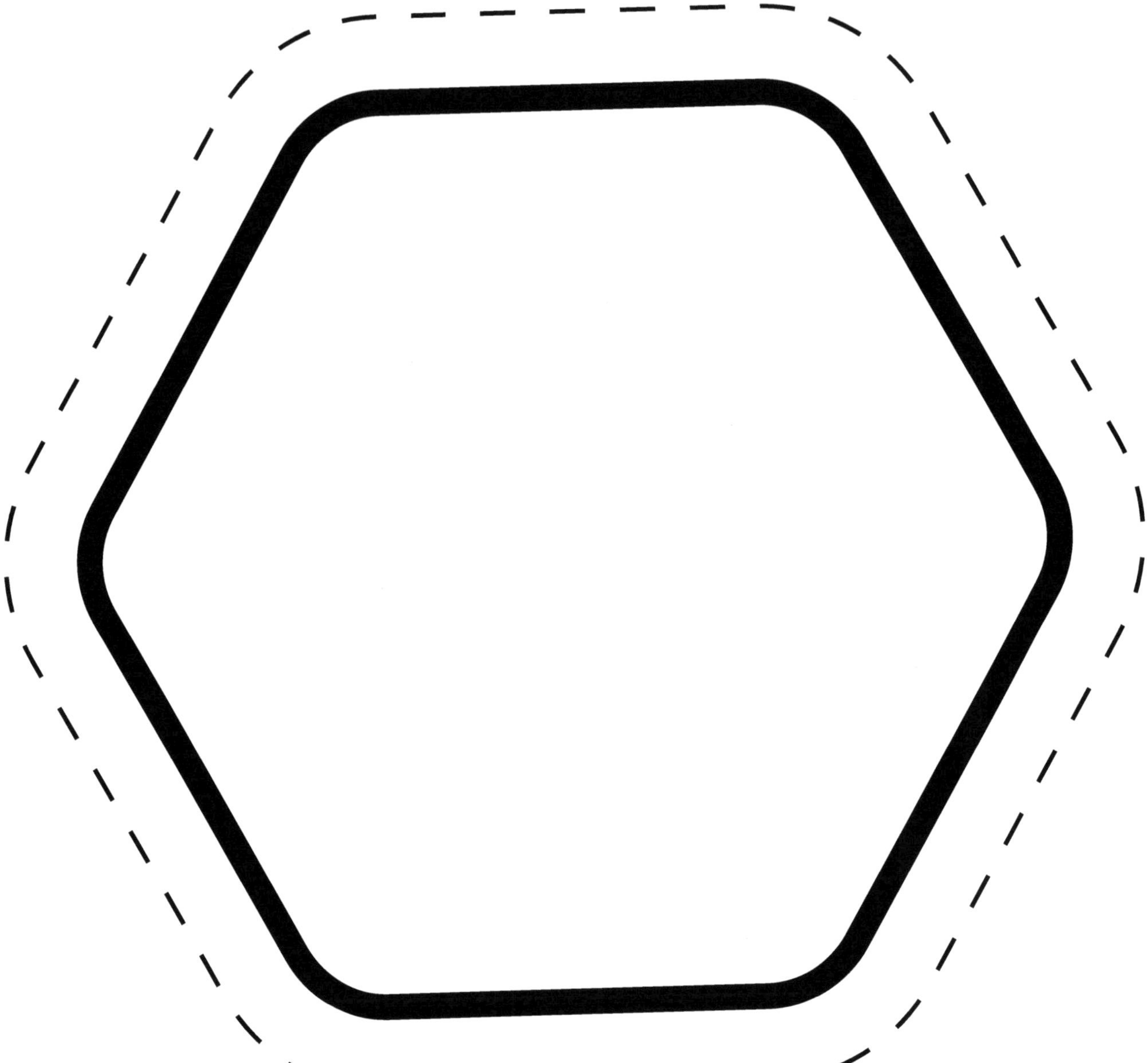

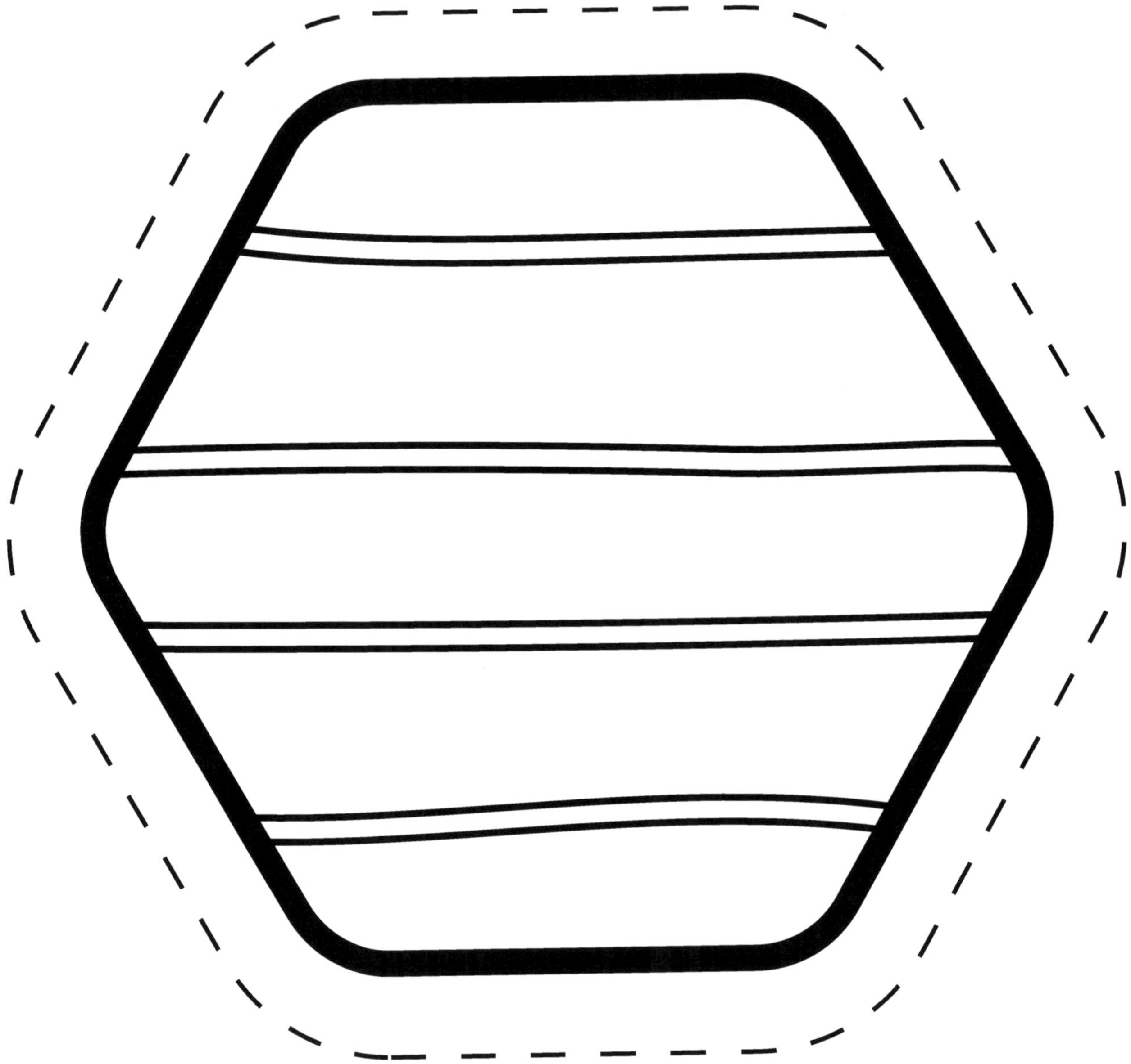

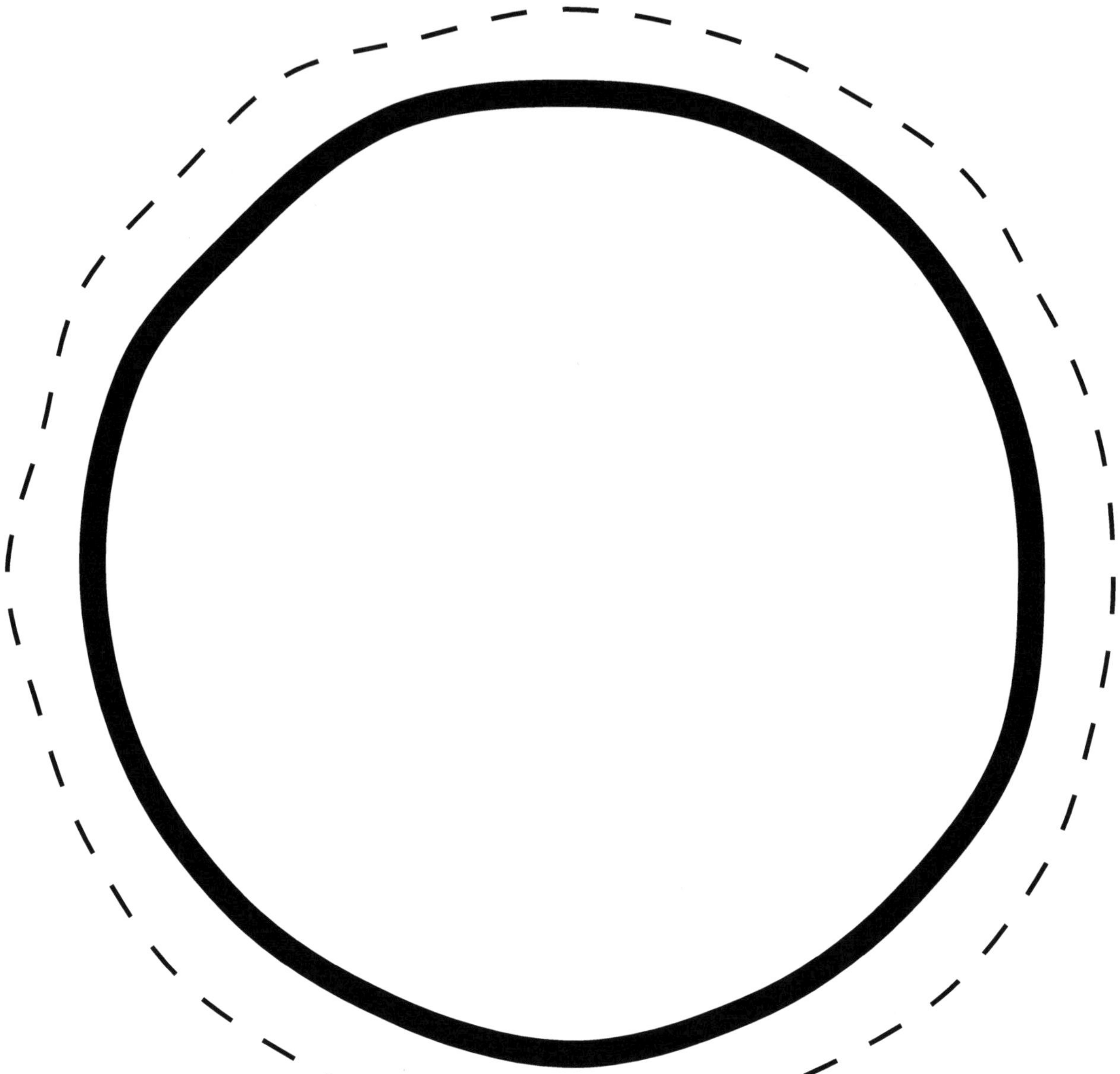

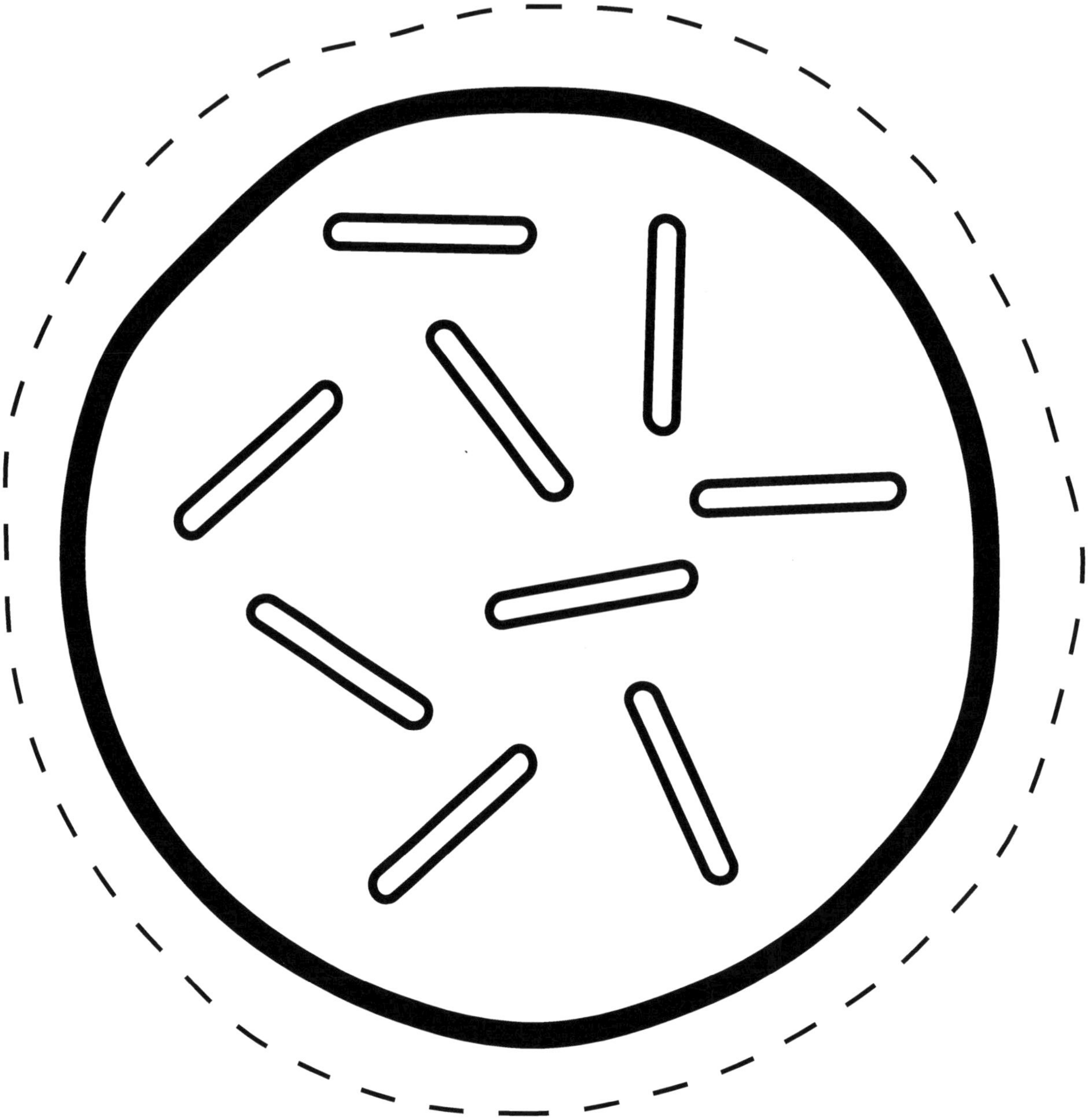

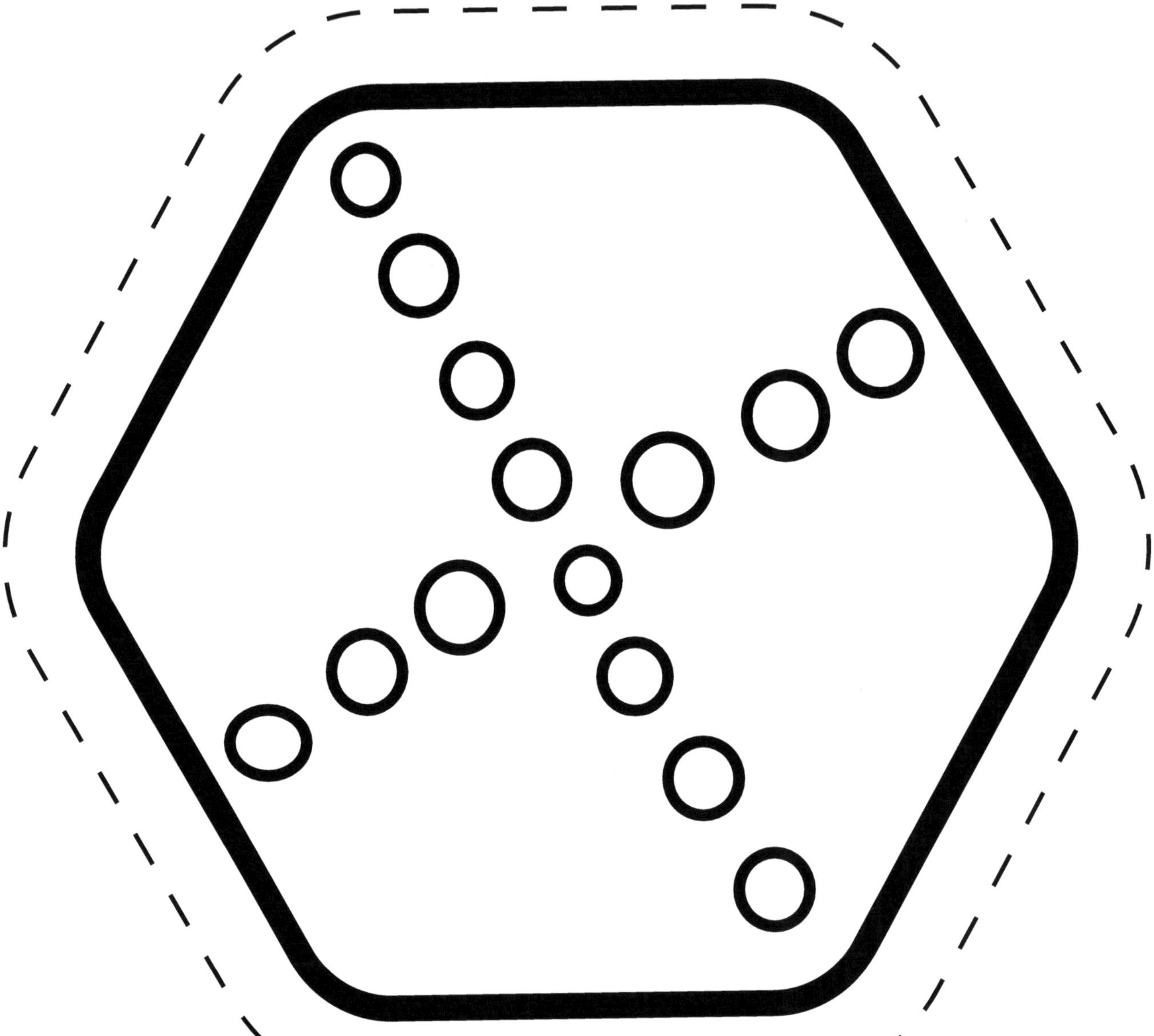

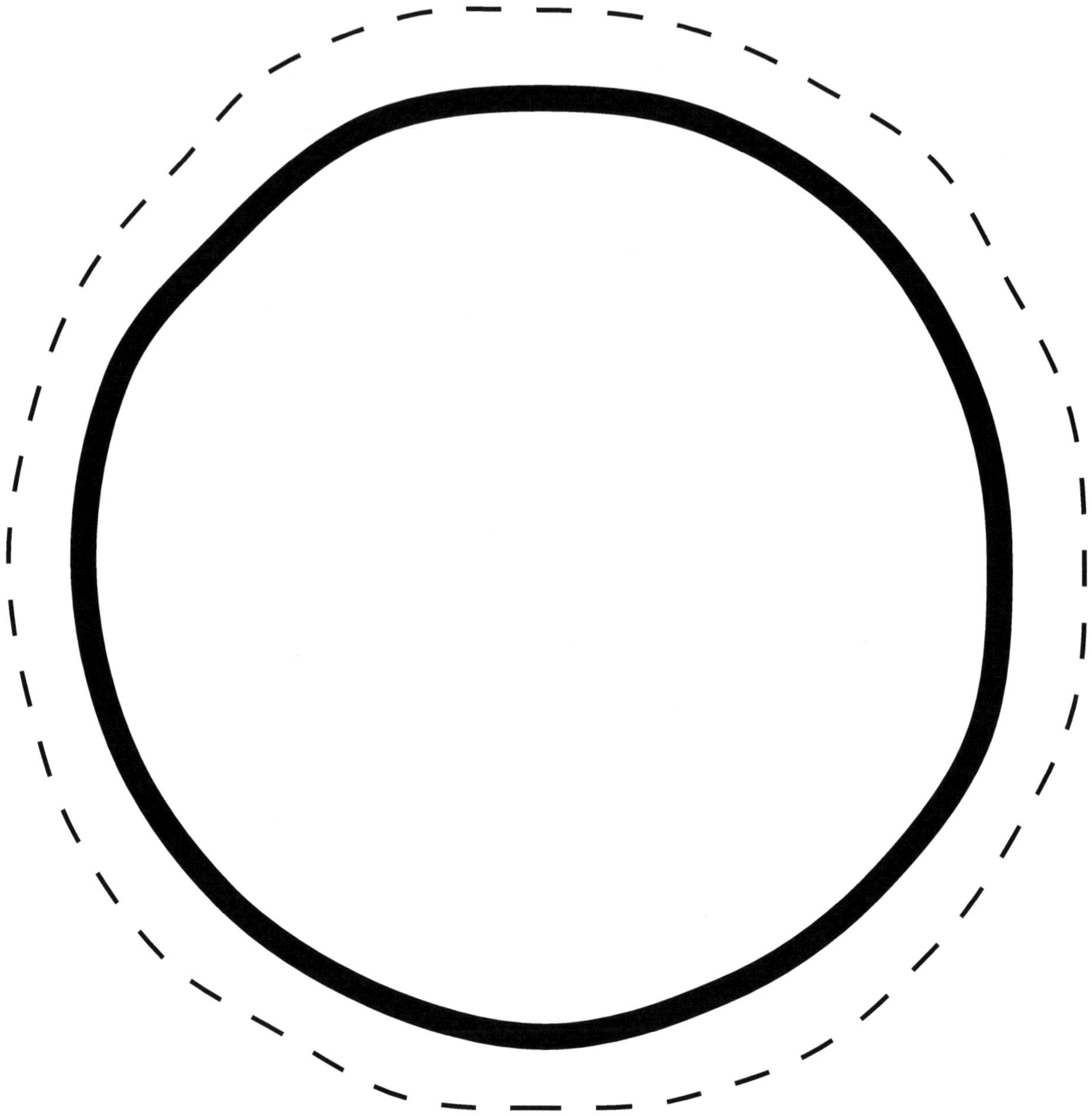

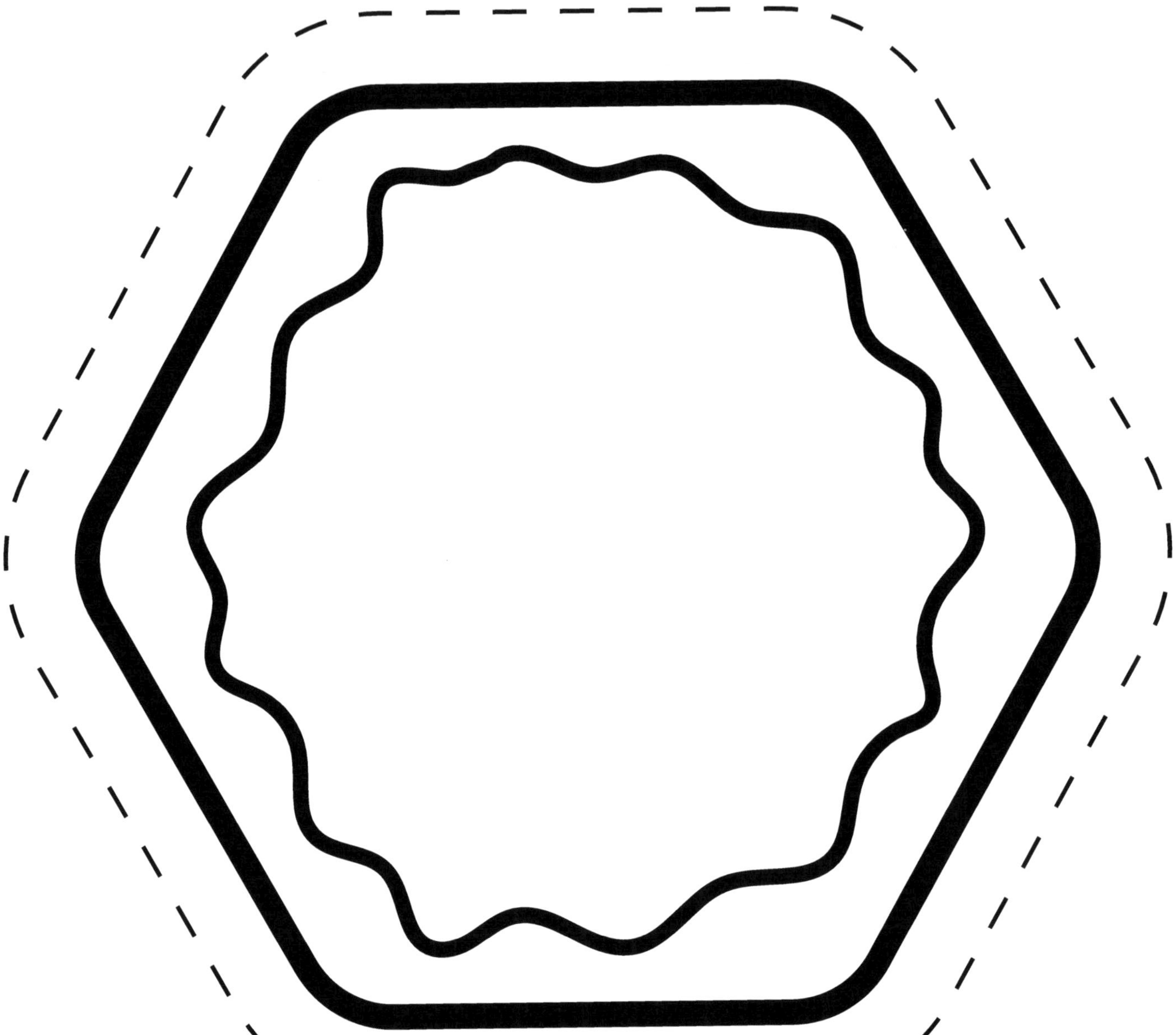

Made in the USA
Columbia, SC
01 November 2022

70311968R10059